I0815635

THE ULTIMATE ANIMAL LIBRARY
Gray Squirrels
by Janie Scheffer
BLASTOFF! READERS
2
BELLWETHER MEDIA • MINNEAPOLIS, MN

Blastoff! Readers are carefully developed by literacy experts to build reading stamina and move students toward fluency by combining standards-based content with developmentally appropriate text.

Level 1 provides the most support through repetition of high-frequency words, light text, predictable sentence patterns, and strong visual support.

Level 2 offers early readers a bit more challenge through varied sentences, increased text load, and text-supportive special features.

Level 3 advances early-fluent readers toward fluency through increased text load, less reliance on photos, advancing concepts, longer sentences, and more complex special features.

★ **Blastoff! Universe**

Reading Level

Blastoff! Beginners — Grade K

Grades 1–3

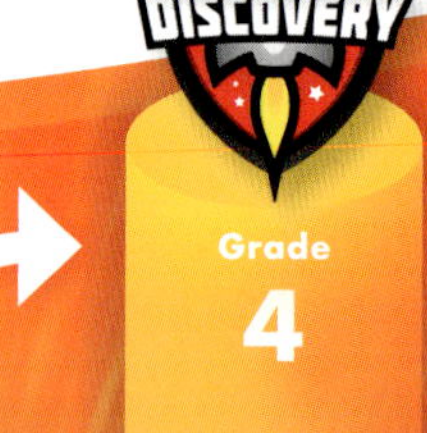

Grade 4

This edition first published in 2025 by Bellwether Media, Inc.

Library of Congress Cataloging-in-Publication Data

Names: Scheffer, Janie, 1992- author
Title: Gray squirrels / by Janie Scheffer.
Description: Minneapolis, MN : Bellwether Media, Inc, 2025. | Series: Blastoff! Readers: The Ultimate Animal Library | Includes bibliographical references and index. | Audience term: Juvenile | Audience: Ages 5-8 Bellwether Media | Audience: Grades 2-3 Bellwether Media | Summary: "Relevant images match informative text in this introduction to gray squirrels. Intended for students in kindergarten through third grade"- Provided by publisher.
Identifiers: LCCN 2024038360 (print) | LCCN 2024038361 (ebook) | ISBN 9798893042399 library binding | ISBN 9798893043365 ebook
Subjects: LCSH: Sciurus carolinensis--Juvenile literature
Classification: LCC QL737.R68 S323 2025 (print) | LCC QL737.R68 (ebook) | DDC 599.36/2--dc23/eng
LC record available at https://lccn.loc.gov/2024038360
LC ebook record available at https://lccn.loc.gov/2024038361

Editor: Elizabeth Neuenfeldt Series Designer: Veah Demmin

Printed in the United States of America, North Mankato, MN.

Table of Contents

What Are Gray Squirrels?

Gray squirrels are well-known **mammals**. They have long, **bushy** tails to balance and **communicate**. These animals mostly live in North America.

Eastern Gray Squirrel Report

Gray squirrels are medium-sized **rodents**.

Their fur is gray. It can be mixed with brown, black, and white.

Gray squirrels have sharp **incisor teeth**. These teeth never stop growing.

These teeth help the squirrels bite through hard foods.

Spot a Gray Squirrel
bushy tail
gray, brown, black, and white fur
sharp incisor teeth
strong back legs

Gray squirrels have strong back legs. They can easily climb trees.

They can jump 6 feet (1.8 meters) up from the ground. They can run 15 miles (24 kilometers) per hour!

Hide and Find!

Gray squirrels live in forests and cities.

They make **dreys**
with twigs and leaves.
Dreys are high up in trees.

Gray squirrels hide food for the winter. They can bury up to 25 nuts in 30 minutes!

Their noses help them find the buried food.

Gray squirrels are **omnivores**.
They mostly eat nuts and berries.
They also eat **insects**.

They have many **predators**. Gray squirrels use their speed to get away.

Growing Up

Female gray squirrels give birth to around two to four **kits** at a time.

Kits are born blind and hairless. Kits can open their eyes about one month later.

kits

Kits leave their mothers after three months. They find their own **territories**.

These high-climbing squirrels can live up to 12 years!

Name of Babies

kits

Number of Babies

around 2 to 4

Time Spent with Mom

Glossary

bushy—thick and fluffy

communicate—to send and receive information

dreys—squirrel nests in treetops; dreys are made of twigs and leaves.

incisor teeth—front teeth used for cutting

insects—small animals with six legs and bodies divided into three parts

kits—baby squirrels

mammals—warm-blooded animals that have backbones and feed their young milk

omnivores—animals that eat both plants and animals

predators—animals that hunt other animals for food

rodents—small animals that gnaw on their food; mice, rats, and squirrels are all rodents.

territories—areas where animals live

To Learn More

AT THE LIBRARY

Chanez, Katie. *Squirrel Kits in the Wild.* Minneapolis, Minn.: Jump!, 2024.

Gagne, Tammy. *Kids' Backyard Safari: Gray Squirrels.* Mount Joy, Pa.: Curious Fox Books, 2024.

Kenney, Karen Latchana. *Forests.* Minneapolis, Minn.: Bellwether Media, 2022.

ON THE WEB

FACTSURFER

Factsurfer.com gives you a safe, fun way to find more information.

1. Go to www.factsurfer.com.
2. Enter "gray squirrels" into the search box and click 🔍.
3. Select your book cover to see a list of related content.

Index

The images in this book are reproduced through the courtesy of: Svetlana Foote, front cover, p. 9; QQQQQQQT, front cover background, interior background; Shabana Yousaf, front cover (squirrel icon); IrinaK, p. 3; Catherine_P, p. 4; Dave Turner, p. 6; Anya Julia, p. 7; Rabbitti, p. 8; Vine.Photographic, pp. 8-9; Bilanol, p. 10; Travis Potter, p. 11; Krtek1, p. 12; Sunshower Shots, p. 13; Nigel J. Harris, pp. 14, 16-17; Orchidpoet, p. 15; Don Mammoser, p. 17 (hawks); Arthur van der Kooij, p. 17 (foxes); Derek R. Audette, p. 17 (coyotes); Tony Quinn, p. 17 (squirrel); SakSa, p. 17 (nuts); Pavlo Lys, p. 17 (berries); Christian Cramer, p. 17 (insects); Gay Bumgarner/ Alamy, p. 18; Annmarie Young Photography/ Getty Images, pp. 18-19; A Turton, p. 20; Carrie Schamberger, p. 21; Aarachchige Don, p. 21 (squirrel icon); Tom Curtis, p. 23.